Brief Encounters

Brief Encounters

*Entertaining Brushes with
the Famous and Infamous*

Sarah Kennedy
With illustrations by Chris Duggan

Headline

First published in 2001 by Headline Book Publishing

10 9 8 7 6 5 4 3 2 1

The publishers have made every effort to be in touch with the contributors to
this book and would be glad to hear from anyone who they have
not been able to contact.

British Library Cataloguing in Publication Data
is available from the British Library

ISBN 0 7472 2771 3

Typeset by Jane Coney
Printed and bound in Great Britain by Clays Ltd, St Ives Plc

Headline Book Publishing
A division of Hodder Headline
338 Euston Road
London
NW1 3BH

www.headline.co.uk
www.hodderheadline.com

*For all Dawn Patrollers and to my BBC colleagues **behind** the studio glass, who often don't get the credit they deserve*

Contents

Introduction

One morning on my BBC Radio 2 Dawn Patrol programme (6-7.30 a.m.), BJ, my cohort behind the glass, for a bit of one-upmanship, said in my headphones: 'Well, that's nothing! When I was three I sat on Yuri Gagarin's knee in Colombo airport.' It happened that the great astronaut, first man in space, was marooned in Ceylon because of a tropical storm. Oh, the irony – go into space, still no cure for the common cold, then get monsooned in a flipping airport! The young BJ had slipped under the security ropes and, naturally, security went ape. But our space hero rocked BJ on his knee and gave him a Russian cosmonaut badge which he still treasures.

His tale opened up the floodgates of *your* memories, some silly, some almost unbelievable (see Jack the Ripper), and some totally bizarre. Why was Bing Crosby in the Lake District at 7 a.m. one fine spring morning, and why does golfer Tiger Woods, worth squillions, owe a Dawn Patroller £5.60? Read on!

This book is about normal bods meeting abnormally famous bods. Hope you enjoy Radio 2's pooled memories, and did I ever tell you when I was in the Ladies and do you know who was in there with me ...?

Sarah Kennedy.

Criminal Connections

Doctor Crippen poisoned his wife and sailed to Canada with his mistress, Ethel le Neve. He was arrested when disembarking from the ship in 1910 and was the first criminal to be apprehended by the use of radio telegraphy.

My most criminal offence was doing an overnight Oxfam walk aged 18. By 19 miles I ended up, exhausted and blistered, at Battersea police station. A policeman offered to drive me back to Sussex and Mother found us having bacon and eggs in the kitchen at 6 a.m. Reflectively, I think he'd had his mind on something other than breakfast ...Thank you, Mother!

[S.K.]

Is there a doctor in the house?

My husband's great-great-uncle was Captain Henry Kendall, the captain on the ship the *Montrose* where the message was received to inform them that they had Doctor Crippen on board.

Mr & Mrs Crellin

Cup final

I have been researching an ancestor of mine – one Melbourne Inman – who was a famous billiards champion in the early 1900s. I discovered from old newspaper articles that he was a somewhat pompous and arrogant man who put fear into his opponents on the billiard tables. In one article mention is made that a Lord Alverstone, the then president of the Billiards Association, had that week sentenced the notorious Doctor Crippen to death and was just handing over the cup to Melbourne when Tom Reece, another famous player of the day, interjected: 'Excuse me, my lord, but if you knew as much as I do about Inman, you would have given Crippen the cup and sentenced Inman to death!'

Carol Tucker

Dicey dentist

My grandmother, who died in 1968, had a tooth extracted by Doctor Crippen!

Keith Moore

Noises from next door

My dad, who was the drummer with a band called Carroll Gibbons and the Savoy Orpheans back in 1900, stayed in a house where the back garden abutted Doctor Crippen's!

Jill Nicoll

Creepy floorboards

My best friend Joan has a friend called Geraldine, whose grandmother was Doctor Crippen's cleaner.

Jay Homer

[Can you imagine it? 'Pay extra attention to the floorboards, please, Annie'! S.K.]

Sweet encounter

My uncle, Roy Stevens, says that when he was a toddler in the mid 1920s, he was in a shop with his mother in Addiscombe, Croydon, when a lady came up to him. She admired his curly hair and bought him a bar of chocolate. After she had gone, the shop assistant said: 'Do you know who that was? It was Ethel le Neve, Doctor Crippen's mistress.'

Angela from Royston

Il Duce

In 1927 a party from our convent school visited Italy. We were summoned by Benito Mussolini himself and had an audience with the Pope and our photograph was splashed over the newspaper *Il Tevere*.

Joyce Holden

A ripping yarn!

My mum's friend Rose, who is over 85, was the youngest of nine children and told me this story a while ago. The family lived in the Aldgate/Stepney area of London, the local street market being Whitechapel. Rose's mother was walking home one dark winter's afternoon from the market, heavily pregnant with her first child, when a very heavy fog descended. The mists, her condition and the sounds of the boats on the river added to her unease and she started to lose her way, getting confused about her surroundings and distressed regarding her advanced condition. To her relief, she saw coming towards her a gentleman whom she described as wearing a top hat, frock coat and carrying a walking cane. She asked for his assistance in finding the right way home and he told her to take his arm and proceeded to walk her right to her street door. She turned to thank him. He replied in a quiet voice, 'Tonight, madam, you can tell your friends and family that you have been brought home by Jack the Ripper.' Startled, she looked round but he had vanished into the fog.

Jean Pearl Brown (Miss)

In the footsteps of the Führer

During a visit to Bavaria I went to the Eagle's Nest, Hitler's retreat at Berchtesgaden. My mother and I both used the toilets where both Eva Braun and Hitler had, as my mother put it, 'wet their whistle'!

Alan Haynes

Gimme shelter!

My grandfather was secretary to the Royal British Legion and in 1938 a group of men from the RBL went over to Germany and my grandfather actually shook hands with Adolf Hitler himself. He wasn't very impressed with Hitler and as soon as he returned home, he built an Anderson shelter in the back garden as he knew war was imminent.

Sis Marsh

Hairy moment
Megan's dad cut Rudolf Hess's hair!

Megan and David Reed

Have you seen this man?
In the 1970s I was lucky enough to have a flat in Eaton Square, London. My next door neighbour was Lord Boothby and just down the road in Lower Belgrave Street were Hayley Mills and Roy Boulting. However, two doors away and also in Lower Belgrave Street was Lady Lucan. On the fateful night of 8th November 1974 [Lady Lucan's nanny, Sandra Rivett, was found bludgeoned to death in the family home in Lower Belgrave Street], as I sat watching *Monty Python's Flying Circus* on TV, I had no idea what was going on only yards from my flat. For several days after that we had the foreign press camped outside hoping to glean more details about the murder.

Mary Guppy

For whom the bell tolls

My father was an officer in the Royal Tank Regiment. In the same regiment were Richard Greene of Robin Hood fame and John Le Mesurier, but by far the most intriguing person was Albert Pierrepoint, the executioner, who, as a sergeant, would approach my father for special leave to go and carry out an execution.

Jenny Odell

Legendary Liaisons

My aunt Gwendoline (sounds reminiscent of *The Importance of Being Earnest*!) was allowing me to stay in London while I was desperately trying to get into broadcasting. Nobody wanted me. Phone rings:

'Agatha Christie speaking. Is Gwendoline in?'

'Oh yes,' says me, 'and I'm Napoleon!' and put the phone down. Two minutes later she rang back and, yes, she WAS Agatha Christie.

[S.K.]

Wild, Wild North

Years ago my father-in-law, 'Daddy Chester', had a pub in Hull called The Rose Tavern and one day who should walk in but Wild Bill Hickok!

Carrie Chester

Crocodile rock

In September 1964 the pianist at my friend Rita's wedding reception turned out to be a young chap named Reg Dwight (who later changed his name to Elton John!).

Sylvia Hurford

A lady descends

My mother was taken to Australia after the First World War and stayed for 18 years. During that time she remembers going to Queensland and standing in a muddy field which was cordoned off by a rope. A little plane landed, and out of it came Amy Johnson, looking very dishevelled. It was her very first landing.

Pat Bradley

My dear old thing ...

A few years back when my son was living at home, I picked up the telephone to be greeted with, 'Brian Johnston here.' Johnners wanted my son to play cricket for the Paul Getty XI and we went to the match on Paul Getty's estate where I met the man himself.

Sheila Stickells

Hat trick

An elderly Swedish friend was on one occasion travelling between Sweden and England, having booked a berth in a shared two-man cabin. He was amazed and delighted to find that his travelling companion was his hero, Stanley Matthews.

Judy Jansson

On Her Majesty's Secret Service

A few years ago I was fortunate enough to be invited to a function held in the Palace of Westminster. After a wonderful meal, my host was kind enough to show me round the House of Commons. While we were sitting on the famous green benches, another MP appeared with his two

The name's Churchill-Winston Churchill

O.H.M.S.

O.H.M.S.S.

guests. My host moved over to greet him and I found myself shaking hands with Winston Churchill and Sean Connery. I still tell people I met James Bond in the House of Commons.

Dave Best

I left my heart in ... Zurich

At Zurich airport my husband and I once met Dr Christiaan Barnard who was on his way home after treating Boris Yeltsin in Russia.

Jenifer Barbakow

Don't sing!

In 1940-41 I was a little girl living with my grand-parents in an apartment in New York overlooking the East River. Every day our cleaning lady would take me across the street to play in the park. Sometimes a man who lived in the building would take me to the park. We would watch the boats on the river, play games and he would push me on the swings. When he was pushing, he would sing. He had a gravelly voice and I would tell him to stop because he didn't know how to sing. I grew up and went to school and never saw the man again. Years later, my grandmother took me to the movie, *The Jolson Story*, and at the first sound of his voice I recognised my friend from the park. My grandmother confirmed that the man who used to take me to the park was indeed Al Jolson.

Judith Durling

They can't take that away from me

When I was about ten I was taken to London to see the sights and to go to the theatre. We went to see a very famous American singer and I was so impressed I insisted on going to the stage door to get my programme signed. The star was very friendly, chatted for a while and signed her autograph. A few days later, we were walking along Bond Street and suddenly, there she was again with her huge smile. 'Hello Pam,' she said, 'we met at the theatre the other night – do you remember? I'm Ella.' Even at the age of ten the irony of Ella Fitzgerald asking if I remembered her was not lost on me.

Pam from Brittany

Special member

When I was little just before the war, every Easter we used to travel to London from Nottingham. On the Sunday we always went to the Zoo, which was then only open on Sundays to members of the Zoological Society or their friends. My father used to borrow a membership ticket from a friend and colleague from one of the London hospitals where he had worked. It was only about 15 years ago, just before my mother died, that I discovered that I used to visit the Zoo on the ticket of the then Dr Alexander Fleming.

Dr Terry Clarke

Stand up straight, Felicity!

I had been visiting relatives in England with my baby daughter and I was a rather fraught young mum. I was at the airport about to return home to Guernsey, when a rather bossy older woman asked if she could be of assistance. I was not as polite as I could have been and even avoided her on the plane. Imagine my utter disbelief and regret when I discovered I had passed up the opportunity to be in the company of the inimitable Joyce Grenfell.

Felicity Kenyon

These boots were made for climbing

One day my husband came home from the local shoe repairer, who was about to retire. There was no one to take over the business and he was selling some of his equipment. My husband was admiring a sewing machine and the cobbler said: 'I'm keeping this – it was my brother's machine and on it he made the boots that Sir Edmund Hillary and his team wore when they climbed Mount Everest.'

Judy Jansson

Death of a sales assistant?

When I was about 24, I was working for Jaeger in
Regent Street, in London. One day there was a bit
of a security scramble and a customer was rushed
into a fitting room. There was a rumour that it
was Marilyn Monroe. The store manager told me
that there was a customer who wanted to see
cashmere jackets, and that I must be discreet.

When I entered the room, there was Marilyn herself and I had to help her choose the right size jacket for Arthur Miller.

Ronnie Gibson

Incidentally

My mum was once housekeeper to Rudolf Nureyev.

André Ferguson

Pas de dust

The kid

When I was a very young child, I was taken to Heathrow airport with my parents and aunt to meet my cousin who was arriving from Geneva. My father left us all standing outside while he fetched the car. While we were waiting, a grey-haired man and a lady joined us, and as they did so they nodded and said hello. A large Rolls-Royce drew up and the couple got in, saying goodbye to us and waving. As they were doing this, several photographers arrived, busily taking pictures of them. My mother asked the photographers who they were, and they replied, 'Didn't you recognise Charlie Chaplin?'

Gay Lander

A truly blithe spirit

Many years ago Noel Coward was at the Liverpool Playhouse and, being a devoted fan, I went round to the stage door to see if I could catch a glimpse of my idol. It was a miserable night, pouring with rain, but suddenly the stage door flew open and there stood Noel Coward himself. He took one look at me and said, 'Come inside at once!' whereupon he handed me a bunch of envelopes and said, 'You may help me open my telegrams.' My hands were shaking as I did so, but he was very amusing as he read them out.

Marjorie Monkhouse

A Brief Encounter

Reversing the charges

During the late 1960s I was dining with some friends at the very fashionable Mirabelle restaurant in London's West End. At the coffee stage of the meal I left the table in search of the Ladies room. Whilst passing through an ante-room to the restaurant, I noticed a small gentleman using the public telephones which were in little individual booths. He was getting extremely angry with the telephone operator on the other end of the line and I heard him say, 'What do you mean, they won't accept the charges? Tell them it's Onassis!' And it was Aristotle Onassis.

Jenny Hebditch

Stan and the slogger

The recent death of our famous Potteries son, Stanley Matthews, reminded me of my father Les's tales of when he went to school with Stan. They were friends and Stan was the top man at school for football and my father was top man at cricket (known as 'slogger'). There was a lot of friendly rivalry between the two and Stan often went back to my gran's house from school with my father for a jam butty. Apparently they used to drive her mad! My father, who has now sadly passed away, only ever reached county cricket and never aspired to the fame of his mate, but he followed Stan's career with great interest and we went to watch his final match. They did meet up again years later and Stan still called my father 'slogger'.

Lynne Smith

A royal delivery

I was born in 1942 in the blackout and the midwife who delivered me was Princess Adimola of Abyssinia (now Ethiopia), daughter of Haile Selassie.

Pat Beaven

Majestic
Meetings

What would you have done in this situation?
On stage for The Prince's Trust Awards, Prince
Charles calls me Jane Kennedy throughout.
Audience titters! He looks perplexed; probably
checks his flies. Do I correct him? No, just keep
on beaming. Afterwards, his equerry invites me
into 'the presence' for him to apologise. I say:
'Edward, it was no problem!' Good man – he
laughed and I enjoyed the weekend in the Tower!
[S.K.]

One's extraordinary dog

In the late 60s I was living in Norfolk and one day was on my way to meet my daughter from school. I had our corgi with us, who was mainly white with a small amount of tan. Suddenly I was aware that a large black car had stopped at traffic lights right beside me. Just then, the rear window of the car rolled down and a voice said, 'What an unusual colour your dog is.' It was the Queen, pointing out my dog to the Queen Mother sitting next to her.

Pamela Henson

The princess and the sausage

A couple of years ago my friend Lyn and I spent a lovely weekend at the Gatcombe Horse trials watching the three-day eventing. We spent a long time looking at a stand selling all sorts of lovely things and decided to come back at the end of the day to get some Gatcombe Old Spot sausages. When we returned to the stand there was nobody there and, just as we were about to go back to our caravan, Princess Anne and her husband drew up in a Land Rover and asked if they could help us. She found some of the sausages under the counter and sold them to us. They were so delicious that we went back the following day and the Princess Royal was there again. We were delighted to have been sold sausages by a princess twice!

Barbara Jones

A sailor went to sea

I served on board the HMS *Hermione* in 1972 with HRH The Prince of Wales. I was a Control Electrical Artificer Apprentice and he was a Sub-Lieutenant. I had to fit the scrambler phone in his cabin, and we both had Special Sea Duty Stations on the bridge where I shared his binoculars on the way into Portsmouth Harbour.

C. C. Heaver (I Eng MIIE)

Heir to the throne?

When Queen Victoria visited the Isle of Wight she would tour her estates in a carriage and often stopped at a particular cottage to use the facilities. The structure was a long wooden box with a hole cut in the middle into which the loo was placed. Some years later, my grandmother moved into this cottage and would often remark that she had put her 'bum' where Queen Victoria had put hers.

Barbara Tye

Knickers and lamplights

My great grandmother used to do all the embroidery on Queen Victoria's underwear and my great grandfather used to be in charge of lighting all the lamps in Windsor Castle.

Jackie Hanington

Only eyes for Sophie

For many years my job has involved travelling to different companies and meeting a lot of people. I always remember faces, but hardly ever names. About two years ago, I was walking down London's Buckingham Palace Road and saw two men walking towards me, one of whom I was sure I knew really well. Not wishing to appear rude, I looked him straight in the eye and gave him a beaming smile. His eyes slid sideways and he moved carefully to the edge of the pavement and hurried past. I then realised it was Prince Edward.

Janice Carter

Rhubarb and custard

The Queen's driving instructor, Mrs Rebecca Harding-Frances, used to give my family rhubarb grown on her country estate.

Matt Bown

A rather grand gardener

When my grandmother was about ten, her father

worked at the local stately home called Luton Hoo. One day she took her father his lunch and there was an old gentleman talking to my great grandfather and helping with the weeding. He asked my grandmother to fetch them some beer from a nearby shop. Having accomplished this task, he gave her a sixpence and she went home. That evening, when her father asked her if she had recognised the man, she said no and was told to look at the sixpence. There was the gentleman's face on the front – Edward VII.

Gayle Walton

Eager punter

Some years ago myself and a group of friends used to go to Cheltenham every year for the festival. One year a friend called Alan was rushing to put his bet on and as he turned the corner he bumped into an old lady, knocking her to the ground. Muttering abject apologies, he helped her get to her feet, along with a lot of other people and continued on his way. After making his transaction, he was walking back to the stand when he heard a group of agitated men talking: 'I tell you, he knocked the Queen Mum over!' Alan, being a staunch monarchist (and the Queen Mother being the patron of the National Hunt), was cursing the clumsy person who did this. It was some minutes before the awful truth dawned upon him.

David Beaton

Ouch!

We are Jewish and both our sons were circumcised shortly after birth. The man who 'did' my elder son also 'did' Prince Charles.

Ursula Markham

The King of Spain's drawers

When my grandson Daniel was three I took him to a local yacht marina for a walk. He suddenly hurtled round a corner with me in hot pursuit and I found him with his face buried in the King of Spain's fly buttons! His Majesty patted Daniel on the head and his bodyguard gently gave him back to me.

Ann Rossiter

The Crown Jewels

Don't you know who I am?

I was a student in Oxford in 1983. I was cycling through the park at Blenheim when an oldish man in a Land Rover stopped me and told me to get off my bike and walk. Being rather miffed – I was miles from the palace at the time and on the tarmac road – I cheekily asked the driver who he thought he was. He calmly said, 'I own the place.' It was the Duke of Marlborough himself.

Andrew Plumridge

A very royal woggle

When I was 11 and in the Sea Scouts, it was Trafalgar Day and the 2nd Fareham Sea Scouts were on parade next to the HMS *Victory* in Portsmouth. I was standing to attention with my new furry woggle (made from a bit of my mother's old fur coat) waiting for the inspection. Imagine our surprise to be inspected by none other than Lord Mountbatten. He didn't make many stops on his inspection, but my furry woggle caught his eye.

Martin Daubney

Shaking hands

Around 1930 my sister, who is 12 years older than me, was pushing me in my pram around the grounds of Pitsford Hall in Northamptonshire. My mother was a housekeeper and my father was a stud groom for a Captain and Mrs Drummond. On this particular afternoon the then Duke of York was calling with his daughter Princess Elizabeth. She asked who the sweet little baby all in white was and the Duke of York told her, 'That's Thorpe's daughter, Barbara Jean.' She came over and shook hands with me but as she would only have been five at the time, she would not remember the incident.

Barbara Leonard

Not the Germans this time ...

About five years ago we went to St Lucia on holiday and, on our arrival, we were greeted by a sprightly charming man in a white dhoti and straw hat who turned out to be Lord Glenconner. Every morning he appeared at breakfast on the verandah. After a few days there was a rumour that Princess Margaret was due to arrive at the hotel and that evening we saw her having dinner with Lord and Lady Glenconner. Next morning after breakfast we took a stroll around the magnificent grounds and were annoyed to see six loungers and two sun umbrellas by the pool had been 'commandeered' with towels. There was a distinct shortage of loungers so I told my husband that if the owners of the towels hadn't arrived by the time we got back, we would take two for ourselves. Half an hour later, we were very surprised to see that the loungers had all been occupied by Princess Margaret and her party – but at least we got to swim with her.

Karen McEwan

A likely story ...
My mother is Queen Elizabeth II and I am the heir to the throne.

Charles Windsor (Karen Hutchins)
[Pull the other one! S.K.]

Foggy meeting

Some 13 years ago I was walking atop Maiden Castle near Dorchester in the fog one November. I was exercising our two dogs and had my two-year-old son, Kye, with me. Through the mist I saw some men standing about on the ramparts dressed in dark suits and trench coats. Further on I saw a group of men walking towards us and, as they got nearer, Kye shouted out, 'Hiya, man!' at the top of his voice. As they reached us, I realised the chap he had shouted to was Prince Charles. He asked if he could intrude and walked round with us, chatting as we went.

Sandy Bromley

Ooh Dr Beeching ...

Many years ago I was on my way by train to Weston-super-Mare. I had to change trains at Bristol and went to sit in the waiting room. There was only one other person, a soldier, in there. After a while the doors burst open and in walked a very distinguished gentleman in a navy cloak and medals, followed by staff and a few family members. The soldier whispered to me, 'Do you know who he is? Emperor Haile Selassie of Ethiopia.'

Mrs Trew

Oops!

My great grandfather used to be a bell boy at the Savoy Hotel and once in the gentlemen's room he dropped a wet sponge on the Czar of Russia's shoes.

Robin Matthews

Charlie's missed calling?

Long ago I was a very young secretary to a doctor whose most famous patients were Prince Charles and Princess Anne. Usually he went to the Palace, but sometimes they came to his consulting rooms in Harley Street. They would arrive with a bodyguard and two nannies. Prince Charles would greet me by name and shake my hand; Anne was two and had lovely golden curls. One day, Prince Charles wanted to see my office and made straight for my typewriter. Quite naturally, I picked him up and sat him on my knee so he could reach the keys. The nannies didn't seem to mind and I liked the thought that the future king was sitting on my knee.

Ann Tauwhare

Old friends

Some years ago I was at Cowes, attending the first ever World Youth Windsurfing Regatta as Principal Race Officer, and using my thirty-two-foot fishing boat as the Committee Boat. With the Regatta over, I was relaxing on board waiting to attend the prize giving, when I was hailed by a very posh motor yacht and realised that it was bringing the guest dignitary for the prize giving – ex-King Constantine of Greece. A couple of minutes later a voice from the jetty said, 'Do you mind if I come across?' and before I could stop them, there was King Constantine standing in the cockpit of my boat shaking hands with the King of Siam!

Tim Hockin

Rear-ended!

In 1977 I was serving in the army at the Royal Military Academy, Sandhurst, as a Regimental Policeman. At the time Princess Anne was married to Captain Mark Phillips and they lived on the Academy grounds in Oak Grove House, which had its own stable block. One of my colleagues, Paddy, was engaged to Susan, who was the Princess's groom, and we often included a visit to the stables whilst out on patrol during our shift to have a chat and a cuppa with Susan. One frosty winter morning at about 6 o'clock towards the end of a night shift, Paddy and I were driving at walking pace past the stables when I saw Susan bending over next to the stable door preparing the horse's feed. I thought I would give her a little scare and trundled up, intending to give her a light smack on the rear as we drove past. Just before the moment of contact, she became aware of something approaching and looked round – it was not Susan, but Princess Anne! I nearly had heart failure and all I could think to do in that split second before contact was to bring my arm up in a salute. I burbled, 'Good morning, Ma'am.' 'Morning,' she replied huffily, and eyed me warily as we drove past. I often wonder what would have happened if I had made contact with the Royal Rear!

David Henley, Colchester

Shaggy dog story

In the mid 1960s a friend and I were walking my labrador in Windsor Great Park. I suddenly heard the dog barking excitedly. Turning round, I saw that she had brought two horses to a halt. I went back to her and bent down to get hold of her collar, saying, 'I'm so sorry, I didn't hear you coming.' Then I looked up at the riders. One was the Queen, the other her bodyguard. They didn't speak, but turned and galloped away.

Beryl Chapman

Royal jazz

My late father was sunk on the HMS *Royal Oak* at the start of the war. Part of his convalescence was in Kandy, Ceylon. Dad was part of Queen Salote of Tonga's Imperial Guard and he also guarded The Temple of the Tooth. He was also often treated to some jazz, which the King of Tonga, a big jazz fan, would play on his saxophone!

Jim Wood

Is that you, Dad?

As a child we lived in Northern Rhodesia (now Zimbabwe) and there was great excitement when the then Prince of Wales (briefly Edward VIII) paid a visit. He loved to escape from his entourage and on this occasion ended up in a bar and got chatting to an old boy called Totty Hay, who said to him: 'Your face is familiar, but I'm unable to put a name to it.' The Prince said, 'I'm the Prince of Wales,' to which Totty retorted, 'If you're the Prince of Wales, I'm your dad!' The following day, the Prince of Wales was inspecting a Guard of Honour comprising a number of Pioneers, who included Totty. The Prince drew level with him and said, 'Hello, Dad!' which sent the crowd mad with mirth.

Teresa Ray Tutt

Is that you, Mummy?

In 1977 I was returning with some friends from an event in Bellahouston Park in Glasgow, during which we had had a fundraising competition for hospital radio to guess how many yards of bandages were wrapped around a shop mannequin in a hospital bed. When we were taking the dummy – still wrapped in bandages – back to the radio studio we realised that the Queen and the Duke of Edinburgh were due to pass by on their way back from an engagement in the city. As they swept along the otherwise deserted street in their glass-topped Rolls-Royce, she in tiara and he in evening dress, the royal party had a very clear view of us, and a slim, mummy-like creature swathed head to toe in bandages who was waving vigorously at Her Majesty and His Royal Highness – and the Duke gallantly waved back, much to our delight. To this day I wonder if they thought it was an escapee from some dreadful road accident.

Mary Buckley (née McConville)

Royal tea break

When Prince William was born the Queen and Prince Charles went together to the hospital to see Princess Diana and the new baby. Police were posted all over the building and one older policeman thought he had the easy job. He was stationed in the basement where the lift came down. Never thinking he would encounter anyone, he was at his post but decided to make himself comfortable by sitting on a box with a mug of tea and his collar loosened. It was quite dark down there, but all of a sudden the lift doors opened and the Queen and Prince Charles were standing there laughing. Apparently, they had pushed the wrong button and went down instead of up. The poor policeman had never stood up so quickly in his life, discarding his tea and trying to straighten himself up, much to the amusement of his royal audience.

Carol Fitzgerald

Pardon?

Several years ago my husband Denis was stuck in traffic in Kensington High Street, London. It was a sweltering day and he was vaguely conscious of a car at the side of him. What caught his eye were some fingers tapping on the side of the door. Then a couple of vehicles in front he noticed an old mate and hooted at him. 'Hi,' shouted the friend. Denis couldn't quite hear and shouted back, 'What's that?' to which his mate shouted back, 'Turn up your hearing aid, you old sod!' When he looked around he saw that it was Princess Diana in the car next to him – she thought these antics were hilarious and had a great laugh.

Carol Fitzgerald

Star Gazing

I'm not one to name drop, BUT ... I witnessed Sir Noel Coward, elegance personified, entering a huge limousine. He had just viewed the film *10, Rillington Place* (based on the notorious 1940s Christie murders – horrors on a par with those of Fred and Rosemary West). On a lighter note, I once tripped on a camera cable and fell on top of Sean Connery! I wished I could have stayed there but, shaken and stirred, I got up and apologised.

[S.K.]

No seats on the bus

During the war I was an evacuee in Keighley, West
Yorkshire, and as the bus to school used to fill up,
a gentleman would often let me perch on his knee
– it was Denis Healey's father.

Dorothy Bisatt

Charmed, I'm sure

Many years ago my twin sons were playing on the beach with a little boy whose father turned out to be the late great Terry-Thomas.

Joan Boyd

A relative moment

Many years ago our friend Gwynith met her friend's uncle outside the main synagogue in Cardiff – he had a thick moustache and wild hair and it turned out to be Albert Einstein.

D.D. Armour

Royal juice

Myself and my son once had a conversation with Princess Diana and a very young Prince William in the local shop in Crathie, Aberdeenshire, about orange juice.

Sharon Conner

Two little boys

Back in the early 1960s I used to work in Lloyds Bank in Cheltenham, which was then full of characters such as colonels and rubber planters who had come home to retire. One old chap used to visit the bank every Thursday at 11, more for a chat than anything else, and always made a bee-line for me. He invariably mentioned that his wife had been Swedish and talked of his time in the army. I took my two-year-old son Jon in one Thursday, as I thought it would be nice for him to meet Mr Sparrow, this wonderful old man. He made much of Jon, who will be able to tell his children that he shook hands with the Drummer Boy who was at theBoer War's Relief of Mafeking.

Richard Darke

A summer outing

My children and I once went to Cliff Richard's house in Weybridge and my eldest son Leigh used his toilet.

Rosemarie A. Strugnell

Childhood companions

When I was a child Matthew Kelly lived around the corner and often used to come and play with my dolls' house.

Gillian Savage, (néeSwann)

Just the girl next door

In the early 1930s in London's East End my aunt, Emma Butler, had aspirations to open a singing/dancing school. She and her friend Vera Walsh sat in the front parlour and planned to achieve their goal. Had it not been for the intervention of the Second World War, they might have succeeded and my aunt might have been as famous as her friend, now known as Vera Lynn.

Jo Stracey

Famous outlaw

In my early teens I used to pick up Richard Todd's arrows while he was practising for the part of Robin Hood.

Eileen Hedges

Cochineal Ken

In the late 1960s I used to scrounge beetles from my neighbour to feed to a tropical fish I had. He kept various amphibians in his bedroom and used these unfortunate insects as food for them, but he would only let me have one at a time. His name was Ken Livingstone.

John Leaver

Do you think I'm sexy?

Many years ago at my friend's house her son and his mates used to gather regularly. One of the lads would be sitting on the settee with a girl on either side, while in the kichen my friend and I would be consoling another girl who couldn't get near him. The name of the young lad was Rod Stewart.

Anne Farnden

An unfair advantage?

I was at Eden Park school in Brixham, Devon, in the early 1970s and our class teacher, Miss Barker, was very popular – all the children adored her. One day she brought her sister to the class for a visit and we all went out to play rounders. When it was the turn of our special visitor to bat, she hit the ball down through the children who parted like the Red Sea. We were all amazed at the batting ability of Jane Barker's sister, who apparently played a bit of tennis and was called Sue.

P.J. Warren

Slowhand's granny

About 20 years ago we lived in Shamley Green, Surrey. I used to catch the bus to Guildford with my young daughter and, while waiting at the bus stop, I often met a sweet old lady and we would chat and laugh while waiting for the bus. One day I asked her where she lived and she replied, 'Just opposite the pub,' and said that her grandson had bought the house for her. I said that he must be very well off to buy her a house and she replied:

'Yes, he is very rich and famous – you may have heard of him. His name is Eric Clapton.'

Rosebud Turk

Encore!

When my sons were very young I decided to take them to see the Trooping the Colour in London. We got on the train and found ourselves in a carriage with Elsie and Doris Waters, both with scripts on their laps. They must have been hoping for a quiet journey, but were very happy to play with my sons.

Joy Horner

Frankly, my dears ...

In the early 1950s my husband and I took two small girls on holiday to Cornwall. It was near Kynance Cove and Gunwalloe Beach and perfect for children to play on the sand and rocks, but only in the mornings. In the afternoons it was occupied by a film company and we often saw Clark Gable there, who was friendliness itself and had his picture taken with us.

Joan Bride

The pursuit of tea

When I was seven my father was working for Lord Redesdale and my sister and I were thrilled to be invited for tea in the nursery with the Mitford girls: Jessica, Nancy, Diana and Deborah.

Iris Hatch

Meeting Miss Marple

When I was a child my mother ran a dressmaking business, and one of her clients was the wonderful actress Margaret Rutherford. I remember that when she came for fittings she often stayed to tea and was very friendly.

Edra Britten

A thoroughly thespian affair

At the outbreak of war my father was head gardener to the Marquis of Headfort at Kells in Ireland. The Marchioness was Rosie Boot, a former 'Gaiety Girl', so theatrical people were frequent house guests there, and were often shown round the lovely gardens. One day my mum nervously lined up my sister and me in our Sunday best to say hello to Leslie Howard and Noel Coward, mum's favourite film idols.

Jennifer Burnap

Rescued by a roller

My elder sister Pauline was a pupil at Mitcham Girls' Grammar School, in London in the 1950s, and one day they were sent home early because of a thick fog. She and her friend were waiting at a bus stop when a Rolls-Royce pulled up and the chauffeur offered them a lift home. They got in and chatted to the man sitting in the back all the way home. When she got home my sister told our mum that she had been given a lift in a Rolls-Royce by a man called Charles Laughton.

Pat Smith

An inside job?

I was a 16-year-old junior in the men's department of Jaeger in Stratford-upon-Avon in 1951. One day during the manager's lunch hour in came Richard Burton. He was then about 25 with that wonderful voice and eyes to die for. I sold him a pair of lovat green socks but then had to call a male sales assistant down to take over, as he needed a pair of trousers and I was not allowed to measure the inside leg. What a chance missed!

Brigid Aita

Out of my depth

My first day at Eton. I was a very small, overawed young boy from Leeds aged 13, away at boarding school for the very first time. As new boys we were blessed with the position of 'fags' to the House Prefects. Basically, we were enslaved; sent on errands, ordered to tidy their rooms and make their coffee – simply to do their bidding. Character-building stuff, we were told. After our first lunch we had to queue up outside the prefects' common room to await our tasks. Although the school had an internal telephone system, it was notoriously unreli-able. E-mail was more than 15 years in the future. So we often found ourselves charged with taking written messages from our masters to similarly important people in other houses. The house captain summoned me forward and presented me with a note to carry to one of his friends in another house. Off I scurried, not really knowing where I was going, but eager to please. I found the other house and, after asking around, found my way to the recipient's room, and a poky little dishevelled room it was too. I handed him the note. He was a tall, handsome and elegant young man of about 17. I remember him smiling at me in a kindly, sympathetic fashion as he composed his response to my house captain's missive. Although our encounter was so very brief, his friendly and engaging nature was very apparent – it must have been in the genes. A few months later he was the most famous boy in the school when his sister Diana became engaged to the Prince of Wales. Such was my brief encounter with Charles Spencer.

Adrian

Toilet humour

Over 30 years ago we were staying in a hotel in Chipping Campden with our two-year-old son, Nicholas. Roy Kinnear was appearing at the Royal Shakespeare Theatre in Stratford-upon-Avon that summer. We were just finishing our lunch in the hotel when Roy Kinnear entered with an elderly lady and sat down at the next table. I went to the ladies' and as I returned down the open staircase, saw my husband collecting our possessions and Nicholas standing near Roy Kinnear. Just then my son saw me and shouted at the top of his voice, 'My mummy has been for a poo!' Needless to say, Mr Kinnear nearly fell off his chair laughing.

Dorothy Bland, Walney Island

Falling Stars

Excepting some politicians, I have found most well-known people extremely courteous and genuine. If *we* were having a cuppa or a glass of wine – well, I'm not one to gossip, but … I'd tell you about AR, SW, KD and JC – you'll never work them out! But *they* are right b*****ds!

[S.K.]

Fancy that!
Noel Coward made a pass at my father!

Tessa Bennett

Feline accident
My wife's granny's cat was run over by Diana Dors many years ago in Dorset.

Mike Barrett

Posh parks
Victoria Beckham was parked outside a post office in Goffs Oak, Herts, badly blocking-in other motorists. When asked if she would move she declined, asking them 'Don't you know who I am?' She did eventually drive off, giving a two-finger salute as she did so – not very posh behaviour.

Audrey Marlow

Three of the best
In 1950-52 I attended Dovedale Road School in Liverpool. My teacher was a Mr Boult and among my classmates were John Lennon, Jimmy Tarbuck

and Peter Sissons. One day I had a fight with John in the playground and bloodied his nose. We shook hands when it was over and that was the end of it. But in class John was ordered to stand up and explain the spots of blood on his shirt. He lied about a nosebleed. Mr Boult pointed out that the penalty for such 'hooliganism' was two strokes of the cane, but if he gave the name of the other boy he would be lenient. John weighed this up and then pointed me out and John got one stroke and I got two!

Anthony Price

Playing hookey

In the mid-1960s my friend Ken and I were bunking off school. We were out exploring on our bikes, when we pulled up at some traffic lights next to a smart limo with dark windows. We were peering nosily into the car and got the shock of our lives when the window was rolled down and we saw The Beatles inside. 'What you doing?' asked John Lennon. We told him we were bunking off school, to which he replied rather gruffly, 'You

kids should get back to school where you belong!'
The car roared off leaving us staring open
mouthed.

Vic Parsons

Unconvincing soldier

I was a young soldier in the early 1960s and,
returning home to Manchester on leave, I went
straight to the Palace Theatre where my dad
worked. I was standing in the wings watching a
rehearsal, when a gentleman pointed in my
direction and said, in a very affected voice: 'I
don't remember a boy in uniform in my play, and
if there was I'd want one that looked like a real
soldier!' The play was *Blithe Spirit* and the gent
who got up my nose was Noel Coward.

John Green

Holy Moses

I used to be a floor manager for a large bookshop
in Birmingham. Soon after I started, Charlton
Heston came in for a book signing for his autobi-
ography. The great man was ushered into the

manager's office and I offered him a tray with three different coffees, teas, mineral water and juices. Without looking at me, he turned to his PA and said, 'Tell him I take cream.' I was so offended that I slammed a cup of black coffee in front of him, said to his PA, 'Tell him we don't have any!' and walked out.

Michael Shortland

Panda-monium!

In the 1960s I took up the enviable position of zookeeper at London Zoo, and among my many tasks I had to look after Chi Chi the giant panda. Chi Chi and I appeared to get on very well for the first three months and then she threw a wobbly and removed my right calf muscle! I was off work for six months but returned to spend six happy years at the zoo. Incidentally, the curator of the zoo at the time was Desmond Morris.

Chris Madden

Mere Mortals' Mishaps

Well, it really did happen. At Royal Ascot I nearly knocked over Her Majesty the Queen. It's true, she's got wonderful skin, but as my 99-year-old aunt says, 'She's never had to wash up, has she?' No comment. Not another weekend in the Tower!
[S.K.]

Dirty look

Edward Woodward scowled at me as my dog peed on his gatepost at Edgehill in Warwickshire.

Fraser Cochrane

Meeting Mr Darcy

My daughter Amy was invited to a Turkish restaurant
in London for supper and during the evening needed
to go to the loo. At the top of the stairs she arrived at the
'convenience' doors only to find both with a picture of
someone wearing a skirt (as in Turkish national dress!).
It was a terrible dilemma, but luckily a gentleman with
a young boy was obviously experiencing the same
problem. Amy and the man then struck up a conversation on which door to choose. After a few minutes of
amusing chat, he said he would go left and she should
go right. Amy realised that the man looked familiar, but
couldn't put a name to the face. Halfway down the
stairs she stopped in her tracks, realising she had just
been talking toilets with Colin Firth, aka Mr Darcy in
the BBC's *Pride and Prejudice!*

Angela Pattenden

Star struck

Whilst running a hotel in Canterbury, Brian Rix
checked in and I was so star struck I forgot to ask
him to sign the register.

Busy Lizzie

The show goes on

In 1958 I was staying at a hotel in München Gladbach, Germany, and my room only had a washbasin; the bathroom was at the end of the corridor. One evening I went to the bathroom and ran a bath. I undressed and, with just a towel round my neck, opened another door expecting to find the toilet. However, sitting at a dressing table, wearing only a bra and pants, was a lady. Quickly I put the towel round my waist, explained in poor German that I thought it was the toilet, and retreated. Later on, I met the same lady in the foyer and she was speaking English. I apologised again and remarked that she looked familiar. She told me that she was Gracie Fields and was there entertaining the troops.

Christopher Weeks

Speak in haste, repent at leisure

As a student in Glasgow in the mid-1980s I used to go to see Scottish Opera productions and get the best seats for about £2. I did this for the premiere of Scottish Opera's production of Leonard Bernstein's *Candide*. He had acted as adviser to this production and was attending with HRH The Duchess of Gloucester. I had a great seat and the production was stunning. In the interval I was standing in the bar when an American voice asked me what I thought of the show. I turned to see an elderly gentleman with swept-back silver hair, wearing a dove-grey shimmering suit and a cream silk shirt – it was quite an image. My first thought, with all the inbuilt prejudice of my early 20s, was 'What a vulgar little man!' and instead of saying what I really thought, I said: 'It's quite enjoyable but I suppose when you've written *West Side Story* everything else is a bit of an anticlimax.' He smiled graciously, said 'Indeed,' and turned away. I returned to my seat for the second half and rose, applauding with the rest of the audience as the Duchess of Gloucester entered the auditorium accompanied by the 'vulgar little man'!

S. W. Fotheringham

Yellow shorts, red face

My wife Cheryl and I used to go to the Val de Lobo in Portugal's Algarve, a favourite haunt of many 'celebs'. Cheryl had bought me some fetching yellow shorts which I was wearing one day. After lunch in a beach shack, I went to the loo which was the size of a telephone box. Because it was so small, I didn't lock the door and when I had finished I fought with the shorts (which included reams of netting material) in the constrained space. At this crucial stage, the door flew open and there stood Judith Chalmers. She jumped back, a look of horror on her face, and disappeared.

The next week I was back home and seeing a friend at the Savoy. As I was walking along the passageway to the restaurant, I saw Judith Chalmers coming towards me. She smiled in recognition, then did a double take and the look of horror returned to her face, while I went a thousand shades of red.

Eric Osborne

'Strewth! Don't you know who I am?

A few years ago while working for *The Sunday Times*, I was in the staff canteen waiting for my cod and chips. The man in front of me was waiting for the same. There were two rather small portions left and, as a new tray of fish was about to arrive, I was happy for this softly spoken, distinguished gentleman to have both the small pieces. The lady behind the counter offered him both pieces for the price of one as they were so small, and he thanked her in his soft Australian accent.

At the checkout, however, the assistant tried to charge him for two pieces of fish. He attempted an explanation, but an argument ensued, getting louder and louder as neither party would budge. Everyone in the canteen was watching by this time. Then came the immortal words: 'You obviously have no idea who I am, do you?' to which the reply came, 'I don't care if you are Rupert Murdoch, you are paying for two pieces of fish!'

Paul Gibbs

Gotcha!

Several years ago Norman Wisdom was staying with us and after dinner, George, our Jack Russell terrier, was sitting on my wife's lap. Norman, as usual, was playing the fool, putting his face closer and closer to George's nose. George waited patiently until Norman was within striking distance, and then sank his teeth into Norman's nose, which poured with blood! Poor Norman had to have a tetanus injection in his backside and still carries the scar on his nose.

Richard Grant

North by North West

Some years ago my husband and I visited Exbury Gardens in Hampshire and we were stunned to spot James Mason walking around. My husband had just purchased a telephoto lens for his new camera and managed to get some very good shots while remaining out of sight. We skulked around dodging behind trees and got at least ten shots. Later we saw him again with some friends and again we got some more photos. Being a big fan, I was really looking forward to getting them developed, but when we got home we discovered that my husband had forgotten to put a film in the camera.

Greta Poulter

Direct hit

In the early 1980s when I was about 12, I was competing in the North of England athletics championships in Gateshead, Tyne and Wear. They had a special guest to present trophies to the winners. I won my race and when it was time for the medal ceremony, they called over the loudspeakers for the first three in my race to go to the box, which was situated above the seating in the stand. I was competing in another race at the time, so I couldn't go immediately. They made several requests for me to go quickly, as the guest of honour was waiting to present me with my trophy. When I'd finished the race I dashed to the stand and began running up the steps two at a time, head down, pulling on the handrail as I swung round the corner. I did not anticipate anyone being round the bend and ran headfirst into the stomach of a man walking with some race officials coming down the other way. He was somewhat larger than myself, so I rebounded off him and bounced down the flight of stairs. The party carried on walking down the stairs and, other than sideways glances of disgust from some of the officials, they took no notice of me in a crumpled heap. No offer of a hand up, or asking after my wellbeing. I picked myself up and cautiously carried on up the stairs. When I got to the top they told me, 'Your medal's over there, you've missed him,' 'Missed who?' I asked. 'Harold Wilson,' they said, 'he's just gone down the stairs – you must have passed him on your way up.' So while I missed out on being presented with my trophy, I can say that I did not miss him!

Jayne Turton

Snookered!

My parents live next door to a holiday camp in sunny Brixham, Devon, and for many years ran the holiday cottages. The house next door is owned by the camp and their managers live in it. My Dad never forgot a face but invariably forgot names, which could be very embarrassing. One day Dad returned from popping next door and told us that there had been a visitor to whom he had said, 'I know you from somewhere, don't I?' The stranger had given him a funny look, and it wasn't until Dad had got home that he realised it was Ray Reardon, who happened to be a good friend of the neighbour. After a while, Ray Reardon bought a house close by, so the sad and terrible persecution visited upon this poor man by my family continued when I was walking along the road with a couple of friends and said in a loud voice, 'Ray Reardon lives there.' We craned our heads up the entrance and, to my horror, came face-to face with the man himself, in his wellies concreting the drive. We gasped and dashed onwards, hoping he hadn't heard!

Kim Griffith

Political Coups

Mine was seeing Sir Winston Churchill in Parliament, as a very elderly, crouched, bulldog figure, still sporting his trademark spotted blue and white bow tie. After he died, my parents took me to his lying in state and it seemed as if most of the nation queued for nearly a day. We kept walking past little white tents which we thought were for Red Cross first aid. After seven hours I eventually wet my knickers. Everyone was there to pay tribute to the great W.C. – all I wanted was to find one!
[S.K.]

Cigar, Sir?

In 1950 I went to the races at Newmarket with my parents and future husband. There was a horse called Colonist II running who had a very famous owner, who duly landed in a small plane. We were among the small crowd waiting and, as he stepped from the plane, he said to us, 'What we want is a bigger majority,' to which my father replied, 'Yes, sir!' The Conservatives had just lost the 1950 General Election. He had a very boyish, pink-cheeked face and looked much younger than I expected Winston Churchill to look.

Sheila Walker

Chips in the offing

In 1957 I was photographed with a former leader of the Labour Party at the official opening of my school. It was the very first purpose-built comprehensive school in London and none other than Hugh Gaitskell was helping me to peel a potato!

Margaret Wogan

What gall!

During the war I worked in Westminster House, London, and part of the building was occupied by the naval section of the Free French Forces. One day a very tall gentleman entered the lift and with a slight bow to me, he touched his cap and said 'Bonjour mam'selle'. I had been saluted by General Charles de Gaulle himself.

Esme Mackins

Oh, mother!

On a family trip to a London exhibition in the 1960s, my mother was told by two uniformed officials not to enter a roped-off VIP area. Mum, who is quite bolshie, bristled with her usual anarchic indignation and proceeded to battle down the forbidden aisle, as we children cringed with embarrassment. As the poor men gently laid hands on her arms to stop her, a smiling new Prime Minister, Harold Wilson appeared before them. As Mum was a great admirer, all was forgiven.

Norma Sykes

Star-Spangled bonnet

In 1960 when I was 11, I was in the car with my dad in Ayr, Strathclyde, when a policeman on a motocycle signalled to us to stop at some traffic lights. We stopped and over the crossroads purred a large shiny black car with a Stars and Stripes on the bonnet. We looked at the man in the back, grinning broadly at us, and realised that by a stroke of luck we had intercepted the cavalcade of President Eisenhower en route from Prestwick airport.

Jim from Stranraer

Top score

My family and friends have a points system for famous people; no points if you have paid to go and see them, but ten points if they make eye contact, touch you and say your name. A ten-pointer eluded us until May 1988 when my four-year-old son, Scott, and I were walking back to our hotel in Durban, South Africa. Nelson Mandela walked out of the hotel, grabbed Scott's hand, asked his name and asked if he could try on Scott's sunglasses.

P. J. Warren

Elementary, Mr President

Some years ago my wife and I met some friends for a drink in the Sherlock Holmes pub near Trafalgar Square, London. After a while we became aware of four well-dressed people with wriggly wires running down the insides of their coats. We wondered whether they were some kind of protection team. Fifteen minutes later, a private door opened and out walked Ronald and Nancy Reagan. They shook hands with us and had a drink before disappearing to the airport.

John Wragg

Brown-eyed girl

When I was a child our garden in Chichester, West Sussex, backed on to the Bishop's garden. We often saw Gandhi walking in the garden and he used to call out to us children perched on the wall. On one occasion years before, my mother had met him in the city and he had looked into my pram and exclaimed, 'What big brown eyes!'

Mary Hill

Use your noodle!

Last August I took my father and son, Matthew, to Beijing for a short holiday. One day, a business friend took us out for the day to see some ancient Chinese temples. Through his interpreter, Mr Zhang told us we would have a surprise for lunch. So, at midday we arrived at what looked like a staff canteen in one of the Ministry of Railways' outlying design institutes. Being the only foreigners there, we caused quite a stir. But the big surprise came when Mr Zhang introduced us to the Noodle Chef. He was a little old man, no taller than about 5 feet 4 inches, and obviously well into his 80s, if not his 90s. He gave us a demonstration of the ancient art of making noodles, mixing the flour and water to make the fresh dough, then twirling it several times until it became the familiar long thin strands of hand-made noodles. The chef then put the noodles into a giant wok of boiling water and served us up a meal fit for a king ... or should I say a president? At this point Mr Zhang's interpreter said: 'This chef used to be the personal Noodle Chef to Mao Tse-tung and Chou En-lai.'

Phil Forgham

Distinguished lift

On my first day, aged five, at a tiny country school in the Scottish Borders there were only two in my year. I was the only boy and I had one girl, Vivienne, as my classmate. The other years were in the same room and included my elder brother and sister, Edwin and Lesley, and Vivienne's sister amongst only a few others. Towards the end of the day I had a little accident in my trousers, having been too shy to ask permission to leave the room. The teacher kindly wrapped the offending trousers ('breeks', in the local tongue) and briefs in brown paper and luckily I had a coat with me for the two-mile walk home. I was very embarrassed and keen to get home, so I happily accepted when my kind classmate offered me a lift in her mother's car, although I was a little worried about ruining their car seats. Along came a lovely grey Volvo. I carefully climbed onto the leather seats and was whisked off home gratefully. My classmate was Lady Vivienne Haig and the driver was Lady Haig senior, wife of Earl Haig.

Lindsay Middler

To Paris with Boris

Back in the early 1980s my brother and I thought we would have a day trip to the Musée de l'Air at Le Bourget, Paris. We took a flight from Heathrow to Charles de Gaulle airport. While walking through the airport we noticed a lot of media activity around one of the lifts. We thought we would hang around to see what was occurring and suddenly all the lights lit up, the lift doors opened and there was Boris Yeltsin. The rest of the day seemed quite insignificant.

Ken Videan

Hi ya, Budgie!

On the Job

While working on the next-door set of *Carry On Matron* at Pincwood Studios, I served Barbra Streisand with a salad.

[S.K.]

An eggy moment

My mother, while working at Cadbury's, once decorated Easter eggs in front of King George VI.

Jane Roberts

No eye contact

After a business meeting in a hotel on the outskirts of Newcastle, I found myself in the gents having a pee next to Liam Gallagher.

Mick Ince

Easy Tiger

About seven years ago, my sister and I were courtesy car drivers for the golfers at the Scottish Open. We were sent to Glasgow Airport to collect two golfers, Tommy Armour and an unknown, Tiger Woods. Having deposited our golfers at their hotels, Tiger Woods and his dad invited my sister and I to have sandwiches and tea with them. They were both very friendly and chatty but it is ironic to think, now that Tiger Woods is so rich and famous, that my sister ended up paying for the sandwiches!

Carolyn and Sandra Johnston

A Batty moment

I was in the Retained Fire Service in Hoyland, South Yorkshire, and we were testing some fire hydrants in the area when we saw two men approaching. When they got nearer to us we recognised them as Bobby and Jack Charlton. We were testing the hydrant next to Big Jack's house. We were having a few laughs with him when a voice came over the wall asking us if we would like a cup of tea. It was Jack's next-door neighbour, Kathy Staff, aka Nora Batty in *Last of the Summer Wine*.

Geoffrey South

Who are you?

During the 1960s I was a gas engineer and was called to a job at a cottage near Reading, Berkshire. The name on the job sheet was 'Daltrey' and when I arrived I was greeted not only by Roger Daltrey himself, but also by Pete Townshend and John Entwistle (Keith Moon was in the States at the time). Being a big Who fan, I was quite overwhelmed and my apprentice and I were well looked after and stayed much longer than necessary! I got all their autographs too which, with the passage of time, I have managed to lose.

Clive Litten

Touch of the William Tells

Thirty years ago I held Sir Norman Wisdom's apple before he went onstage at the Alex Theatre, Birmingham.

Glenys Hackett

Corrr!

Moore, moore, moore

In 1984 I won a trip to see the Prix de l'Arc de Triomphe in my job as a car salesman. At the start of the trip we spent the night at a hotel at Heathrow to catch an early flight. My wife and I decided to have a nightcap in the bar and while standing at the bar a man came and stood next to me. I turned to him to exchange pleasantries and found it was the late great Bobby Moore, who was a delight and ended up buying us drinks.

David Abbott

All the wrong digits

As a young veterinary surgeon, I moved to a new house near Reigate, Surrey. My wife and I had conscientiously put our new telephone number on the answering machine. However, I had managed to get one digit wrong and only discovered the mistake several hours later. So I phoned the number I had left on the machine and was surprised to be speaking to André Previn. He was very charming and most amused when I explained the situation to him.

W. W. Sim

Bring me sunshine

In the 1970s my employer, an American PR company, sent all its executives for a health check. I duly reported to the BUPA place in King's Cross, London, was shown into a cubicle and changed into a gown. Thus clad I returned to the waiting area and sat down. Almost immediately another cubicle opened and out stepped Ernie Wise, who came and sat next to me. I couldn't help glancing down, whereupon Ernie said, 'Yes, they are short, fat and hairy!'

Peter Walker

Driving Miss Handl

My most memorable claim to fame was when the late Irene Handl was appearing at the Beck Theatre in Hayes, Middlesex. I popped her in my car afterwards and drove her to some friends for tea before the evening show. I felt so honoured to have such a famous bottom on my passenger seat that I was loath to sell my Ford Fiesta when the time came!

Daphne Wood

Someone else's chopper

My uncle was a pilot based at Manchester airport for many years. Then he worked for a helicopter company and taught trainee pilots the science of flying. One person he got to know very well and taught to fly a helicopter was Adam Faith.

Lynne Jackson

Hoover groover

Many years ago I was working in an electrical shop and was asked to take a vacuum cleaner to demonstrate at a customer's house. The house was in Esher in Surrey and it was large and surrounded by a high wall. After gaining entry I was ushered into a room and greeted by George Harrison and his wife. They bought the cleaner for the large Indian rugs they had hanging on the walls, and I always hoped it would go wrong so I could call back.

Barry Robinson

A well-conditioned actor

About 12 years ago I was called to repair some air conditioning in the penthouse suite of a hotel in Kensington, London. The unit was duly repaired, but what a shock when the guest returned – it was Douglas Fairbanks Jr., who was very pleased that the job was done. He then sent his 'man' across the road for some cold beers for us. What a gentleman.

Ken Coppard

A salubrious tea party

I used to fly for BOAC as a cabin steward and on one occasion I had to be flown back to London from Mexico City. As the economy class cabin was full, my seat was in first class and in due course a very nice lady sat next to me. We chatted away and after a couple of hours it dawned on me that she looked familiar. I was puzzling over where I knew her from and eventually I asked: 'Do you work for BOAC in London?' 'Oh no, dear,' came the reply, 'I'm Merle Oberon and I'm going to London for Noel Coward's birthday party'!

Terry E. Smith

A saintly visit

Some 25 years ago my husband was senior police officer at a police station in Denham, Buckinghamshire. It was just before Christmas and, as I was passing the station, I looked in to see if my husband could meet me for lunch. His secretary told me I could go straight to his office as his 'special guest' had just left. Intrigued, I walked into his office and the 'special guest' was still sitting there in a pair of dark glasses. He introduced himself as 'Roger ... Roger Moore.' I found out later that his father had been a policeman and each Christmas he visited the local nick to continue his links with the police.

Mrs Jenny Mackie

Bucket thief

A friend of a friend called Sue from Liverpool used to work in the Munich Hilton, West Germany. One day she was looking for something and knocked on a door, but received no answer. Thinking the room was empty, she entered to find a very handsome gentleman in a big white fluffy dressing gown. She looked him in the eye and asked, in her finest Brookside accent: ' 'Ave you got my bucket?' Needless to say, he told her he had not taken it. When asked, 'Are yer sure?' he laughed out loud and assured her he was telling the truth. 'Well, if you 'aven't gorrit, someone else must of robbed it!' It wasn't until she closed the door that she realised she had just been addressing Omar Sharif.

Reverend Gary Wah

Munificent stars

In the early 1970s I was working as a nanny in Hampstead. I joined a local choir and we went carol singing at Christmas. We were very surprised to be singing outside the house of Richard Burton and Elizabeth Taylor. They both came out and Richard Burton gave us £5!

Jan Hills

Nearly a white Christmas

One morning I was driving to work through Cockermouth and as I was going past a pub called The Trout I saw, standing in the doorway, Bing Crosby. Unknown to me, he was on a fishing trip in Cumbria. The town was deserted, there was only me and Bing, but I just drove straight on! It must have been the shock, but I will regret it for the rest of my life.

Jo Graham

Evening, all!

In the late 1950s I was working in Park Lane and there was a London Transport strike. I was only 20 and full of bravado so I thumbed a lift from the first car I saw. It stopped and a very nice man in a trilby took me all the way to my door. It was only during our conversation that I realised he was Jack Warner from *Dixon of Dock Green*.

Anne Bromfield

Shopping list

After leaving school I worked in a builders' merchant/ DIY shop in Claygate, Surrey. Being in the Esher area, we were used to seeing the odd famous face or two. One day in walked a blonde bombshell, 30-something, wearing tight black trousers, a white polo-neck jumper and knee-high black leather high-heeled boots. With a number of 16 to 18-year-old males in attendance in the shop, you can imagine that testosterone levels were soaring. The conversation went thus.

Me: 'Can I help you, Madam?'

Woman: 'Yes, I would like a DUREX colour chart, thank you.'

Silence, then multiple footsteps exiting to the back

room to the sound of smothered laughter and coughing.

Me: 'Yes, Madam, here is your DULUX colour chart. Is there anything else I can help you with?'

Maintaining total control during this exchange was difficult. The customer was looking rather confused at my stress on the work 'Dulux', and looked at the bag she was holding, which was from the chemist across the road. It was at this moment that comedienne Julia McKenzie turned a delightful shade of red and left the shop.

Malcolm Perry

Bank Clark

As a 16-year-old in 1943 I was employed at the Bank of England. One day traversing one of the many corridors, I saw three American servicemen in front of me, and one held the door open for me to go through. I was wearing a tiny gold dollar on a chain round my neck and one of the men commented on it. I looked up and found myself face to face with Clark Gable.

Molly Badger

Not a lot of people know that

During the 1960s my dad was travelling up North by train on business and he was getting rather annoyed with all the girls giggling and pointing in to his carriage. He knew that it couldn't be him they were looking at, as he was an engineer – not a breed normally associated with sex appeal – so it must have been the other chap in the carriage. He resorted to the only training for the professional in these situations and raised his copy of the *Daily Telegraph* higher and harrumphed. By Watford he had had enough of the giggling girls and spoke to the chap.

Dad: 'I say, what is this all about?'

Chap: 'It's me, I'm afraid.'

Dad: 'Well, who are you?'

Chap: 'My name is Michael Caine and can I buy you lunch?'

Malcolm Perry

Poster shock

It must have been 1969 or 1970 and I was newly arrived in London from Nottingham. I had landed what I thought would be an interesting job as a nanny to the daughter of an American businessman and his wife living in Hampstead. I loved the area, especially the Heath. I often went for a walk with my charge, Joy, to the children's play area where parents would bring their children to enjoy the open space and relatively fresh air. One day we went there as usual, but the place was absolutely deserted, except for a lone man and his child. I sat on the bench next to him. He gave me a friendly smile and I smiled back, but nervously because he reminded me of somone I thought I knew. I looked again and felt my face freezing in amazement. This face was on a poster on my bedroom wall – it was Allan Clarke of The Hollies.

Jan Hills

The Young Ones

My husband was a cinema manager and often received invitations to previews of films. In the early 1960s we were invited to a preview of *The Young Ones* starring Cliff Richard. He was there for a photo opportunity and my husband and I were asked to have our photo taken with him. Cliff very politely asked my husband if he would mind if he put his arm around my shoulder. Having received permission, he did and I still have the photo to prove it. My young daughter, who was eight at the time, was absolutely green with envy when she heard about it and saw the picture, as Cliff was her number one heart-throb.

Joan Pettit

Coincidentally

I have long been a devotee of the novels of Thomas Hardy and have never forgotten a very striking BBC television production of *The Mayor of Casterbridge*, shown about 20 years ago and starring the excellent Alan Bates as Michael Henchard and Janet Maw as his wife, Susan. At a conference I attended recently, I was astonished to find myself sharing a table with Janet Maw's mother.

Ruth Rymell

More than keen!

About ten years ago I was working as a planned maintenance inspector for a local authority in Somerset. It was my job to go round the local housing stock and inspect the external fabric of the buildings. I was working in the village of Marston Magna and had to carry out an inspection on a bungalow. I was greeted at the door by a very well-dressed lady and, after a brief chat, I got on with the inspection. When I got round the back of the bungalow her husband was working in the garden and asked me if I would take a look at the damp in the bathroom. As I was walking to the bathroom I noticed that the dining room wall was covered in pictures of Diane Keen (she of *Rings on their Fingers* and the Nescafé ads fame in the 1970s). I said nothing and noted the damp in the bathroom. As I was leaving, I said to the lady that she must be a great fan of Diane Keen's and she replied, 'I hope so – she's my daughter!' I was so embarrassed, but this was compounded by the lady asking if I would like to meet Diane who was in the sitting room. To say I nearly died of embarrassment is an understatement.

Martyn C. Giles

Starlight Express!

A couple of years ago the company that I worked for had a major supplier in Leeds. Living in the south meant regular trips on the GNER service from King's Cross to Leeds. On one trip, four of us had gone to Leeds and in the evening we were taken out for a curry and more than a few beers. In the morning after our meeting, feeling absolutely terrible, we left for London on the

12.05. All was not well aboard the dining carriage. I had a terrible stomach ache and after a while (no delicate way to put this) I needed the loo. My colleagues were eating, so, not wanting to announce my predicament, I silently walked to the loo at the end of the dining carriage. Again, there is no easy way to put this, but I had an upset stomach. After I had finished I washed my hands and opened the door to leave, only to be greeted by none other than Sir Andrew Lloyd Webber! I was so shocked that I didn't have time to suggest that he would do well to find another loo, and he went in locking the door behind him! Highly embarrassed, I returned to my colleagues hoping that they hadn't noticed – but they had, and I endured jibes about the nature of Andrew Lloyd Webber's next musical all the way back to London.

Steve Jarvis

Odds and Ends

Well, we all know a few of these, eh? I once overheard Dame Kiri Te Kanawa (diva) saying to Suzi Quatro (pop singer with pizazz) 'Well, dear, your voice is the Morris Minor, whereas mine is the Rolls-Royce!' They both dissolved into hysterics.

[S.K.]

Another eggy moment

In 1964 I was an apprentice chef in a hotel in Filey, North Yorkshire, and I boiled an egg for Ringo Starr's breakfast.

Colin Buck

Thoroughly Modern Millie

When I was a young girl we met Millicent Martin's grandfather in a car park on the Isle of Wight.

Barbara Faulkner

Nature calls

I was at university in the late 1960s and at a Moody Blues gig I had a pee in the gents in between John Lodge and Justin Hayward!

Kev

Bond and the barmaid

In the 1960s I was a barmaid at a hotel in Christchurch, Dorset, called The King's Arms and I once sat on the stairs talking to Sean Connery.

Joan Collie

Not like Steptoe!

At a garden fete in the Forest of Dean many years ago I met Wilfrid Brambell who invited me to smell the rose in his button-hole.

Mrs J. Wallace

I like it!

I served Gerry Marsden of Gerry and the Pacemakers with anti-wrinkle cream for his stage appearance in Paignton, Devon.

Jennifer M. Burtoo

Woof!
My cousin's daughter's fiancé's guide dog is a half-sister to David Blunkett's guide dog!

Jane Roberts

Not a lot of people know this either
In the early 1960s, my boyfriend, Doug, shared a flat with Michael Caine and Terence Stamp. I can remember one occasion when we all emptied out our pockets to see if we had enough money to go to the local Italian bistro for supper – hard to believe now!

Paddy Howard

Can't get no .... recognition
About four years ago a friend and I were on holiday in Toronto, staying with my daughter. One day we were walking in Edwards Park when two male joggers came along. I noticed one was a young, gorgeous, blond chap and as I was looking at him admiringly he gave me a huge beam. After they had disappeared, my daughter, who is not easily impressed, said, 'Never any

eye contact with him.' I couldn't think what she meant until my friend asked, 'Was that Mick Jagger?' For days afterwards my daughter had great joy in telling her friends that I had been so busy admiring the trainer that I had not even noticed Mick.

Kathleen Dickson

Cleaning for 'old blue eyes'

My partner Fred's mum, Maud, used to be Frank Sinatra's maid.

Jill Sewell

Twist and shout

In the early 1960s I was a student in Dowsefield Lane, Liverpool, which runs parallel to Menilove Avenue and while running for a bus one day I got my 3-inch-stiletto heel stuck in a grating. A male hand grasped my ankle and helped me to heave my foot clear. I thanked him in a hurry and dashed for the bus again and it was only after that I realised it was John Lennon.

Helen White

Strange purchase

In the 1970s I had a Saturday job in Marks &
Spencer in Eastbourne, Sussex, and once sold a
nightie to Fyffe Robertson.

Ruth Rymell

Shop shock

My wife's mother once gave a shopping trolley to
Alvin Stardust's auntie.

Doug Kilborn